# Buildings

JILL FORAN

**WEIGL PUBLISHERS INC.**

**Project Coordinator**
Tina Schwartzenberger

**Design**
Janine Vangool

**Layout**
Bryan Pezzi

**Substantive Editor**
Heather C. Hudak

**Copy Editor**
Jennifer Nault

**Photo Researcher**
Wendy Cosh

Published by Weigl Publishers Inc.
350 5th Avenue, Suite 3304
New York, NY USA 10118-0069
Web site: www.weigl.com

**Library of Congress Cataloging-in-Publication Data**

Foran, Jill.
  Buildings / Jill Foran.
      p. cm. -- (American symbols)
Includes index.
Summary: Uses easy-to-read text to introduce some public buildings in the United States that serve as symbols of the ideals of freedom, justice, and loyalty, such as the United States Capitol and Independence Hall.
  ISBN 1-59036-132-6
  1. Architecture--United States--Juvenile literature. 2. Historic buildings--United States--Juvenile literature. [1. Architecture. 2. Historic buildings.] I. Title. II. Series.
  NA705.F66 2003
  720'.973--dc21
                                    2003005033

Printed in the United States of America
1 2 3 4 5 6 7 8 9 0   07 06 05 04 03

**Photograph Credits**
Every reasonable effort has been made to trace ownership and to obtain permission to reprint copyright material. The publishers would be pleased to have any errors or omissions brought to their attention so that they may be corrected in subsequent printings.

**Cover:** The U.S. Capitol (Bruce Leighty); **Carroll Museums, Inc.:** page 17M; **CORBIS/MAGMA:** pages 4T, 14T (Royalty-Free), 6/7 (Kelly Harriger), 7B (Dennis Degnan), 15B (Robert Holmes), 16T (Thomas A. Heinz), 16M (Joseph Sohm; ChromoSohm Inc.); **Corel Corporation:** page 14B; **Getty Images Inc.:** pages 10/11, 13B; **Bruce Leighty:** pages 1, 3, 8/9, 15T, 16B; **Photos.com:** page 23; **PhotoSpin Inc.:** page 12/13; **Courtesy of the Save Lucy Committee Inc., Margate, NJ. All Rights Reserved. http://www.lucytheelephant.org:** page 17B; **Jim Steinhart of www.PlanetWare.com:** pages: 4B, 5T, 5B, 9T, 11T, 15M, 17T, 22.

# Contents

# Introduction

There are millions of buildings in the United States. These buildings come in different shapes and sizes. They also serve many purposes. There are houses for people to live in, churches for people to worship in, and office buildings for people to work in. There are museums, shopping malls, and theaters. There are also restaurants, schools, and stadiums. Some buildings in the United States are hundreds of years old. Others are newly built.

The Pentagon site in Washington, D.C., covers 583 acres. The building itself takes up 29 acres.

The White House was the first public building built in Washington, D.C.

Many of the country's buildings are important national symbols. These buildings represent something about the United States. They stand for the **ideals** of freedom, justice, and loyalty. Among the best-known national buildings are Independence Hall, the Supreme Court Building, the U.S. Capitol, and the White House. Each of these buildings stands for the ideals of the United States.

The design of the Supreme Court Building was inspired by classical temples.

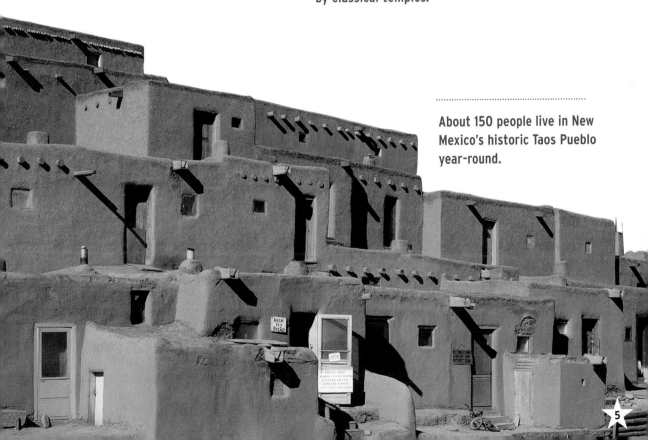

About 150 people live in New Mexico's historic Taos Pueblo year-round.

# Independence Hall

Independence Hall is the birthplace of the United States. This special building is located in Philadelphia, Pennsylvania. It was built as the Pennsylvania State House. Construction began in 1732. At that time, the United States was not yet a country. Pennsylvania and the other states were **colonies** of Great Britain. When Independence Hall was completed, it was one of the largest buildings in all the colonies.

Some of the United States's most important historic events have taken place at Independence Hall. In 1776, colony leaders held an important meeting at Independence Hall. These leaders were the Founding Fathers of the United States. Inside the Assembly Room, they adopted the Declaration of Independence. This document, or paper, stated that the thirteen colonies wanted freedom from British rule. Years later, when the United States was a country, another important meeting was held at Independence Hall. This time, state leaders gathered in the Assembly Room to **debate** and write the Constitution of the United States. The Constitution explains how the government of the United States works. The leaders signed the Constitution at Independence Hall on September 17, 1787. Independence Hall is a World Heritage Site.

Independence Hall is located in Independence National Historic Park. Twenty buildings in the park are open for the public to tour.

# DID YOU KNOW?

★ It took more than twenty years to build Independence Hall.

★ For many years, the basement of Independence Hall served as Philadelphia's dog shelter.

★ The Constitution was written at Independence Hall during the summer. Although it was very hot, the windows in the Assembly Room were nailed shut so that no one could overhear the leaders planning.

★ Independence Hall was home to the Liberty Bell for more than 200 years.

★ The design of the United States flag was chosen at Independence Hall in 1777.

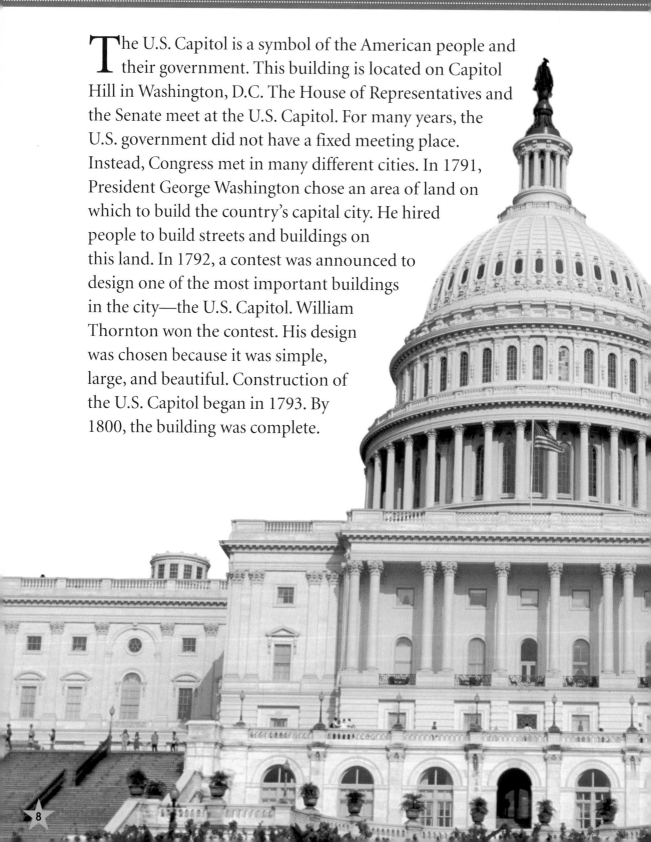

# The U.S. Capitol

The U.S. Capitol is a symbol of the American people and their government. This building is located on Capitol Hill in Washington, D.C. The House of Representatives and the Senate meet at the U.S. Capitol. For many years, the U.S. government did not have a fixed meeting place. Instead, Congress met in many different cities. In 1791, President George Washington chose an area of land on which to build the country's capital city. He hired people to build streets and buildings on this land. In 1792, a contest was announced to design one of the most important buildings in the city—the U.S. Capitol. William Thornton won the contest. His design was chosen because it was simple, large, and beautiful. Construction of the U.S. Capitol began in 1793. By 1800, the building was complete.

Since 1800, many changes have been made to the U.S. Capitol. Today, the building has a central section and two **wings** that extend north and south. The Senate meets in the north wing, and the House of Representatives meets in the south wing. A cast-iron dome, which is a large circular roof, tops the central section. A statue of a woman stands on top of the dome. This statue represents the freedom of the American people.

**The National Statuary Hall is located inside the U.S. Capitol. The hall contains statues of important Americans from all 50 states.**

★ The U.S. Capitol is made mostly of white marble.

★ There are 540 rooms in the U.S. Capitol.

★ The north and south wings of the U.S. Capitol have special rooms where visitors may watch Congress in **session**.

★ The Rotunda is a circular room under the dome. This room is used for important ceremonies and events. It is more than 95 feet wide across the center of the circle, and 183 feet high.

★ Not only is the U.S. Capitol home to the U.S. government, it is also a museum of American art and history.

# The White House

The White House is one of the country's most honored buildings. It is the home of the president of the United States. The president and the presidential staff work in the White House, too. The White House is located in Washington, D.C. It is more than 200 years old. In 1790, President George Washington decided to create a presidential home. A contest was held to find the best design for the house. An American architect named James Hoban won the contest. His design was chosen because it was practical and stately.

Construction of the White House began in 1792. Although George Washington supervised the building of the White House, he did not live in it. He died in 1799—one year before the White House was complete.

The first president to live in the White House was John Adams. John Adams and his wife, Abigail, moved to the White House in 1800. The White House has become an important symbol of the presidency and of the United States government.

**All of the American presidents except George Washington have lived in the White House.**

★ The White House's address is 1600 Pennsylvania Avenue.

★ The White House has 132 rooms, 35 bathrooms, and 6 floors. The president lives on the second floor.

★ The largest room in the White House is the East Room. It is used for state receptions and balls.

★ The president works in the Oval Office, an egg-shaped room inside the White House.

★ Throughout history, the White House has also been called the President's House, the Executive Mansion, and the President's Palace. It was officially named the White House in 1901.

# The Supreme Court

The Supreme Court Building is a symbol of **justice**. It is home to the Supreme Court of the United States. This is the highest court in the country. The Supreme Court Building is located across the street from the U.S. Capitol. It has housed the Supreme Court of the United States since 1935. Before 1935, the Supreme Court did not have its own building. In the late 1700s, the Supreme Court met in New York City and in Philadelphia. When the U.S. government moved to Washington, D.C., the Supreme Court moved, too. For more than 100 years, the Supreme Court met inside the U.S. Capitol.

In 1929, it was decided that the Supreme Court needed its own building. An architect named Cass Gilbert was asked to design the building. Made mainly of marble, the Supreme Court Building has beautiful carvings and large columns, or pillars. Rooms inside the building include the Supreme Court Chamber, a large library, and offices for the justices. The motto "Equal Justice Under Law" is etched above the main entrance of the building.

Sixteen marble columns support the main entrance of the Supreme Court Building.

★ The two main doors at the entrance of the Supreme Court Building are made of bronze. Each door weighs 6.5 tons.

★ A marble figure sits on either side of the building's main steps. On the left side is a female that represents the **Contemplation** of Justice. On the right side is a male figure that represents the **Authority** of Law.

★ The main corridor, or hallway, of the Supreme Court Building is called the Great Hall. This hallway leads to the Supreme Court Chamber.

★ Above the entrance of the Supreme Court Building is a sculptured group of figures representing Liberty Enthroned guarded by Order and Authority.

# More Buildings to Know

From unusual homes to towering offices, many buildings serve as symbols of freedom, justice, and the creativity of the American people. Fascinating **architecture** can be found across the United States.

## ★ The Pentagon

The Pentagon is one of the largest office buildings in the world. It is located in Arlington, Virginia, and is a symbol of **military** power. The Pentagon is the headquarters, or main office, of the United States Department of Defense. The country's air force, army, and navy all have offices in the Pentagon. The building is in the shape of a pentagon, or a five-sided object, and five roads surround the building site.

## ★ The Empire State Building

The Empire State Building is located in New York City, New York. It is one of the country's best-known skyscrapers. A skyscraper is a very tall building. The Empire State Building stands 102 stories high and measures 1,250 feet from the ground to the roof. When it was completed in 1931, it was the tallest building in the world. Today, there are many skyscrapers that are taller than the Empire State Building.

## ★ The Sears Tower

The Sears Tower in Chicago, Illinois, is the tallest skyscraper in North America. Completed in 1973, the Sears Tower is 110 stories high. It measures 1,454 feet from the ground to the roof. The Sears Tower is 2 city blocks wide and weighs 445 million pounds. It is so big that it requires the same amount of electrical power as a town of 35,000 people. There is an **observation deck** on the building's 103rd floor.

## ★ The Space Needle

The Space Needle is located in Seattle, Washington. The tower stands 605 feet tall and is known for its strange shape. The tower looks like a spaceship standing on large, steel legs. The Space Needle was built for the 1962 World's Fair, which attracted millions of tourists. They visited the new tower and rode the elevators to the top. Many tourists still visit the Space Needle. At the top of the tower, there is a **revolving** restaurant and an observation deck. Visitors can look down at the people on the ground from this height.

## ★ Cathedral of St. John the Divine

The world's largest cathedral, the Cathedral of St. John the Divine, is located in New York City, New York. Construction of the building began in 1892. Although it is only two-thirds complete, the cathedral has been open to the public since 1941. At 146 feet wide and 601 feet long, the Cathedral is longer than two football fields. The outside of the church is decorated with beautiful stonework and stained glass windows.

## ★ Fallingwater

A fascinating house in western Pennsylvania is called Fallingwater. An American architect named Frank Lloyd Wright designed the house. Fallingwater is **anchored** on a rock ledge and hangs over a beautiful waterfall. The building is made of concrete, glass, and sandstone. The outside of the house is designed to look like the rock ledge on which it sits. Fallingwater is an example of how a building can blend with nature.

## ★ Cape Hatteras Lighthouse

The Cape Hatteras Lighthouse is located on the Outer Banks of North Carolina. It is the tallest lighthouse in the United States. It stands 205 feet high. For more than 130 years, this lighthouse has guided ships through a dangerous stretch of the Atlantic Ocean. The lighthouse is made of more than 1 million bricks. People began to worry that the sea would wear down these bricks. To stop this from happening, the heavy lighthouse was moved a safe distance inland, away from the water.

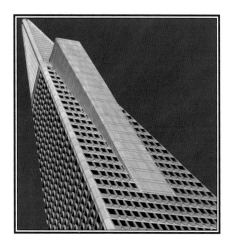

## ★ Transamerica Pyramid

The Transamerica **Pyramid** is located in San Francisco, California. It looks like a pyramid with wings. In 1968, the president of a company named Transamerica decided to build a new office building. He did not want this building to look like other skyscrapers. Instead, he wanted it to be narrow at the top and wide at the bottom. This allows sunlight to reach the streets below. The building stands 853 feet tall and has 48 floors. The fifth floor is the widest.

## ★ Taos Pueblo

Taos Pueblo is located near the town of Taos, New Mexico. The word *pueblo* is Spanish for "village." The Taos peoples built the village more than 600 years ago. It is one of the oldest structures in the United States. Taos Pueblo is two groups of houses that are built from sun-dried mud bricks. Mud bricks are used to build many homes in New Mexico. The buildings of Taos Pueblo have many levels. The upper levels can only be reached by ladder. Taos Pueblo is the oldest **inhabited** Native-American village in North America.

## ★ Phoenix Shot Tower

The Phoenix Shot Tower is located in Baltimore, Maryland. It was built in 1828. Shot towers were used to make bullets for rifles. To make bullets, liquid lead was dropped from the top of the tower into a tub of cold water. The lead droplets would cool and harden into bullets as they fell into the water. Today, there are only four shot towers in the United States. The Phoenix Shot Tower stands more than 234 feet tall. It was the tallest building in America until the Washington Monument was completed in 1884.

## ★ Lucy the Elephant

In 1881, a 65-foot wooden elephant was built in Margate, New Jersey. A real-estate salesperson named James Rafferty designed this peculiar building. He hoped people would come to see it and buy land in the area. For more than 120 years, people have visited this building. About 1 million pieces of lumber, 12,000 feet of tin, and 200 boxes of nails were used to build Lucy the Elephant. The elephant's body is divided into rooms. Visitors reach these rooms by climbing stairs inside the elephant's legs.

# Buildings Everywhere

There are special buildings in many cities and towns across the United States. This map shows the location of the buildings mentioned in this book. Are any of the buildings featured in this book located in your state? If not, try to think of a building in your state that should be placed on this map.

AMERICAN SYMBOLS

1. **Cape Hatteras Lighthouse**: Outer Banks, North Carolina

2. **Cathedral of St. John the Divine**: New York City, New York

3. **Fallingwater**: Mill Run, Pennsylvania

4. **Independence Hall**: Philadelphia, Pennsylvania

5. **Lucy the Elephant**: Margate, New Jersey

6. **Phoenix Shot Tower**: Baltimore, Maryland

7. **Taos Pueblos**: Taos, New Mexico

8. **The Empire State Building**: New York City, New York

9. **The Pentagon**: Arlington, Virginia

10. **The Sears Tower**: Chicago, Illinois

11. **The Space Needle**: Seattle, Washington

12. **The Supreme Court**: Washington, D.C.

13. **The U.S. Capitol**: Washington, D.C.

14. **The White House**: Washington, D.C.

15. **Transamerica Pyramid**: San Francisco, California

# America's State Capitols

Every state in the country has a state capitol. Some states have had more than one capitol. These buildings all have special features and designs. Each building is a symbol of American **unity** and freedom. Find your state capitol on this chart.

| STATE | FEATURES |
| --- | --- |
| Alabama | Completed in 1851; stands 119 feet tall |
| Alaska | Completed in 1931; is built with limestone taken from southeast Alaska |
| Arizona | Completed in 1900; has a 16-foot zinc statue named *Winged Victory* |
| Arkansas | Completed in 1915; covers 287,000 square feet |
| California | Completed in 1874; has granite walls |
| Colorado | Completed in 1908; has a gold-plated dome |
| Connecticut | Completed in 1879; is built of marble and granite |
| Delaware | Completed in 1933; stands 90 feet tall |
| Florida | Completed in 1977; stands 322 feet tall |
| Georgia | Completed in 1889; is one of the first buildings to have elevators |
| Hawai'i | Completed in 1969; is an open-air structure |
| Idaho | Completed in 1920; stands 208 feet tall |
| Illinois | Completed in 1888; took 20 years to build |
| Indiana | Completed in 1888; has a stained-glass dome in the rotunda |
| Iowa | Completed in 1886; has five domes |
| Kansas | Completed in 1903; stands 304 feet tall |
| Kentucky | Completed in 1910; stands 210 feet tall |
| Louisiana | Completed in 1932; is the tallest capitol in the U.S., at 450 feet tall |
| Maine | Completed in 1831; stands 185 feet tall |
| Maryland | Completed in 1779; is the oldest state capitol still in use |
| Massachusetts | Completed in 1798; stands 59 feet tall |
| Michigan | Completed in 1878; stands 267 feet tall |

| | |
|---|---|
| **Minnesota** | Completed in 1905; stands 223 feet tall |
| **Mississippi** | Completed in 1903; has 750 lights in the building's dome |
| **Missouri** | Completed in 1917; has a 30-foot wide staircase |
| **Montana** | Completed in 1902; has a copper-covered dome |
| **Nebraska** | Completed in 1932; is shaped like a **Greek cross** |
| **Nevada** | Completed in 1870; has an octagonal, or eight-sided, dome |
| **New Hampshire** | Completed in 1818; stands 150 feet tall |
| **New Jersey** | Completed in 1792; stands 143 feet tall |
| **New Mexico** | Completed in 1966; is shaped like the Sun |
| **New York** | Completed in 1899; has walls that are more than 16 feet thick |
| **North Carolina** | Completed in 1840; is shaped like a cross |
| **North Dakota** | Completed in 1934; stands 241 feet, 8 inches tall |
| **Ohio** | Completed in 1861; stands 158 feet tall |
| **Oklahoma** | Completed in 1917; stands 155 feet tall |
| **Oregon** | Completed in 1938; was built using four types of marble |
| **Pennsylvania** | Completed in 1906; has a dome that weighs 52 million pounds |
| **Rhode Island** | Completed in 1904; has 15 million bricks |
| **South Carolina** | Completed in 1840; took 56 years to complete |
| **South Dakota** | Completed in 1910; stands 161 feet tall |
| **Tennessee** | Completed in 1859; has a central, square tower that stands 198 feet tall |
| **Texas** | Completed in 1888; is the largest of all state capitols |
| **Utah** | Completed in 1916; the outside is made from quartz |
| **Vermont** | Completed in 1859; has the oldest, non-restored chambers |
| **Virginia** | Completed in 1788; has a new building built around the original building |
| **Washington** | Completed in 1928; weighs 74,500 tons |
| **West Virginia** | Completed in 1932; the outside walls were built from Buff Indiana limestone |
| **Wisconsin** | Completed in 1917; has the world's fourth-largest dome |
| **Wyoming** | Completed in 1917; stands 146 feet tall |

# Further Research

There are many buildings in the United States. Most of these buildings have fascinating histories. Many more have become symbols of American ideals. Several Web sites and books provide information about these buildings.

**Visitors can climb 832 steps to reach the SkyCity Restaurant. The restaurant is at the top of the Space Needle in Seattle, Washington.**

## Web Sites

★ To learn more about your state's capitol, visit:
www.architectsattic.com/state%20capitols.htm

★ To see facts about some of the country's most important buildings, visit:
www.pbs.org/wgbh/buildingbig/wonder

★ To learn more about other state symbols, visit:
www.50states.com

## Books

★ Britton, Tamara. Independence Hall. New York: Checkerboard Library, 2002

★ Curlee, Lynn. Capital. New York: Atheneum, 2003

# Your Favorite Building

Buildings are everywhere. People live, work, and play in buildings. Some people may admire a building because it has an unusual design. Others may like a building because it is a reminder of something special. Do you have a favorite building? Try to think of a few buildings in your neighborhood that are important to you. What makes them special? What do they symbolize? On a large piece of paper, draw a picture of a building you think is special. Next to the picture, write a story about why this building is important to you.

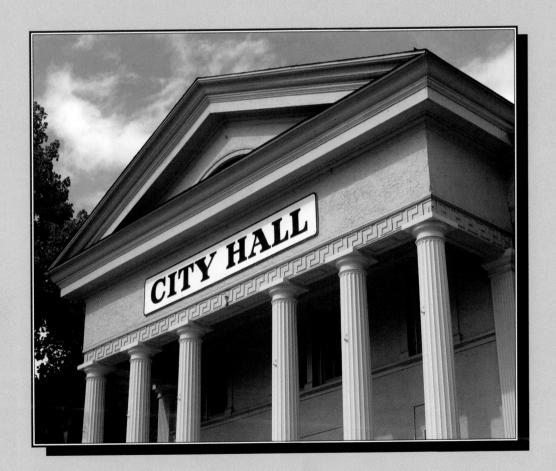

# Glossary

- ★ **anchored:** held down
- ★ **architecture:** the art and science of designing and making buildings
- ★ **authority:** a person who has the right to control something
- ★ **colonies:** areas that are ruled by other countries or states
- ★ **contemplation:** to think about something for a long time
- ★ **debate:** to argue or discuss a question or issue with others
- ★ **Greek cross:** a cross where both bars are of equal length
- ★ **ideals:** principles; high standards
- ★ **inhabited:** lived in
- ★ **justice:** fair and right treatment
- ★ **military:** concerning the armed forces
- ★ **observation deck:** a place, usually at the top of a building, where people can view their surroundings
- ★ **pyramid:** a structure with a square base and triangular sides that meet to form a point at the top
- ★ **revolving:** moving in a circle around a central point
- ★ **session:** a meeting of a group of people
- ★ **unity:** being together
- ★ **wings:** extensions on the sides of a building

# Index